A Squirrel's Story

By Candace H. Haigler

Illlustrated by Jacqueline Decker

Amy the squirrel lived in an elm in the forest. Her nest was perched on a branch at the top. It swayed in the wind.

Then during a storm, the wind tore Amy's nest apart. She tried not to cry about it. Now she must build a new home.

Perhaps, Amy thought, she should visit other homes to get ideas. Why did her friends live in those places? What if one of them was a better home for her?

Amy scrubbed her gray fur, curled her tail over her back, and scurried away.

Helen the frog lived on a lily pad in a sunny pond in the center of the forest.

"My home has plenty of flies and other bugs for me to catch!" exclaimed Helen.

Helen's home was the wettest, muddiest spot. Amy wanted a neater, drier home.

Jason the cricket lived in a crack in a stack of bricks at the back of a garden.

"My home is hot and dry," Jason chirped. "I can stretch out and sing."

Amy squinted into Jason's home. It was too stuffy. She wanted a windier place.

Roger the skunk lived in a large hole under a pile of stones by the forest border.

"My home is safe, and I can forage in the forest after dark," explained Roger.

Roger's home was the draftiest place. Amy wanted a snugger home than that.

Edith the snail was not hard to find because she left a trail of sticky slime.

"My home is the shell I balance on my back," Edith replied. "I carry it with me."

Amy stroked Edith's shell. It was too snug. She wanted a more open home.

Amy squatted by the elm to think. Her friends'
homes were perfect for them. But they felt very
strange to her.

"Bricks, stones, shells, and pads are not
squirrels' homes. I will stay in my elm and build
the biggest, grandest nest ever."

And Amy started that very day.